KEEPSAKES

for the Heart

KEEPSAKES
for the Heart

MOTHERS

Compiled by Alice Gray

Multnomah® Publishers—Sisters, Oregon

PRESENTED

to

Mother's Love

Youth fades; love droops;
The leaves of friendship fall—
A mother's love
outlives them all.

—Oliver Wendell Holmes

CONTENTS

When You Thought I Wasn't Looking

When you thought I wasn't looking, I saw you hang my first painting on the refrigerator, and I wanted to paint another one.

When you thought I wasn't looking, I saw you feed a stray cat, and I thought it was good to be kind to animals.

When you thought I wasn't looking, I saw you make my favorite cake just for me, and I knew that little things are special things.

When you thought I wasn't looking, I heard you say a prayer, and I believed there is a God I could always talk to.

When you thought I wasn't looking, I felt you kiss me goodnight, and I felt loved.

When you thought I wasn't looking, I saw tears come from your eyes, and I learned that sometimes things hurt, but it's all right to cry.

When you thought I wasn't looking, I saw that you cared, and I wanted to be everything that I could be.

When you thought I wasn't looking, I looked…and wanted to say thanks for all the things I saw when you thought I wasn't looking.

—Mary Rita Schilke Korzan

Mother Earned Her Wrinkles

According to her height and weight on the insurance charts, she should be a guard for the Lakers.

She has iron-starved blood, one shoulder is lower than the other, and she bites her fingernails.

She is the most beautiful woman I have ever seen. She should be. She's worked on that body and face for more than 60 years. The process for that kind of beauty can't be rushed.

The wrinkles on her face have been earned... one at a time. The stubborn one around the lips that deepened with every "No!" The thin ones on the forehead that mysteriously appeared when the first child was born.

The eyes are protected by glass now, but you can still see the perma-crinkles around them. Young eyes are darting and fleeting. These are mature eyes that reflect a lifetime. Eyes that have glistened with pride, filled with tears of sorrow, snapped in anger and burned from loss of sleep. They are now direct and penetrating and look at you when you speak.

The bulges are classics. They developed slowly from babies too sleepy to walk who had to be carried home from Grandma's, grocery bags lugged from the car, ashes carried out of the basement while her husband was at war. Now they are fed by a minimum of activity, a full refrigerator and TV bends.

The extra chin is custom-grown and takes years to perfect. Sometimes you can only see it from the side, but it's there. Pampered women don't have an extra chin. They cream them away or pat the muscles until they become firm. But this chin has always been there, supporting a nodding head that has slept in a chair all night...bent over knitting...praying.

The legs are still shapely, but the step is slower. They ran too often for the bus, stood a little too long when she clerked in a department store, got beat up while teaching her daughter how to ride a two-wheeler. They're purple at the back of the knees.

The hands? They're small and veined and have been dunked, dipped, shook, patted, wrung, caught in doors, splintered, dyed, bitten and blistered, but you can't help but be impressed when you see the ring finger that has shrunk from years of wearing the same wedding ring. It takes time—and much more—to diminish a finger.

I looked at Mother long and hard the other day and said, "Mom, I have never seen you look so beautiful."

"I work at it," she snapped.

—Erma Bombeck
from Forever Erma

Act of Love

The story is told of the mother who came home after a long hard day. Her little girl ran out of the house to greet her. "Mommy, Mommy, wait until I tell you what happened today." After listening to a few sentences, the mother responded by indicating the rest could wait as she needed to get dinner started. During the meal, the phone rang, then other family members' stories were longer and louder than the little girl's. Once again she tried after the kitchen was cleaned and the brother's homework questions were answered, but then it was time for her to get ready for bed.

The mom came to tuck her little girl in and quickly listened to her prayers. As she bent down to tousle the little one's curls and to kiss her soft cheek, the child looked up and asked, "Mommy, do you really love me even if you don't have time to listen?"

—*Alice Gray*
from Stories for the Heart

The Nest

Our front door slammed open and shut many times over the years, but there was one summer it was silenced—the summer before the last of our three children left for college. Christine, John and Jeff had been fun to raise and the delight of my life. Even the thought of them leaving home felt empty.

One day, I noticed a mother bird feverishly making a nest on the light fixture by our front door. Twigs and debris were scattered on the ground underneath. Somewhat anxious brown eyes peered quietly over the edge at me.

From that time forward, the front door was off limits. Through the entire active summer, with two kids home from college and another one preparing to leave, everyone used the kitchen door. Soon, the nest burst into activity with the arrival of three little birds. We were able to watch from the kitchen as the mother bird fed and fluffed her babies, cleaned out the nest

and eventually taught them to fly. And then one day, they were gone.

I thought about the mother bird and how her care and tending had ended as the birds flew away leaving nothing but a nest. From the moment I counted the three birds, I began identifying with the whole process, so I carefully took the abandoned home down from its perch and placed it on a shelf in the garage. As I watched Chris and John and now Jeff pack to leave home, I wept realizing the inevitable had come; I had raised my family and it was time for them to apply all the lessons home had taught them.

Late in October of the same year, an unusually loud thunderstorm hit our area. I looked out the kitchen window at the sky and a movement caught my eye. There, huddled under the eaves by the front door, near the porch light, were three fledgling birds. I'm sure it was "our family," returning to find shelter in the only place they knew for sure was safe, familiar, welcoming— because it was home.

Smiling, I returned to my breakfast, knowing I'd been given reassurance. Though the years of nurturing were over, the years ahead would bring many opportunities for sheltering our family. When the crisis, the frightening, the difficult or the overwhelming times come, there is one place that will always be safe, familiar, welcoming for my family—home.

—*Evelyn Petty*
from Stories for the Family's Heart

Treasure

Richer than I you can never be
I had a mother who read to me.

—Anonymous

Come Home

The small house was simple but adequate. It consisted of one large room on a dusty street. Its red-tiled roof was one of many in this poor neighborhood on the outskirts of the Brazilian village. It was a comfortable home. Maria and her daughter, Christina, had done what they could to add color to the gray walls and warmth to the hard dirt floor: an old calendar, a faded photograph of a relative, a wooden crucifix. The furnishings were modest: a pallet on either side of the room, a washbasin, and a wood-burning stove.

Maria's husband had died when Christina was an infant. The young mother, stubbornly refusing opportunities to remarry, got a job and set out to raise her young daughter. And now, fifteen years later, the worst years were over. Though Maria's salary as a maid afforded few luxuries, it was reliable and it did provide food and clothes. And now Christina was old enough to get a job and help out.

Some said Christina got her independence from her mother. She recoiled at the traditional idea of marrying young and raising a family. Not that she couldn't have had her pick of husbands. Her olive skin and brown eyes kept a steady stream of prospects at her door. She had an infectious way of throwing her head back and filling the room with laughter. She also had that rare magic some women have that makes every man feel like a king just by being near them. But it was her spirited curiosity that made her keep all the men at arm's length.

She spoke often of going to the city. She dreamed of trading her dusty neighborhood for exciting avenues and city life. Just the thought of this horrified her mother. Maria was always quick to remind Christina of the harshness of the streets. "People don't know you there. Jobs are scarce and the life is cruel. And besides, if you went there, what would you do for a living?"

Maria knew exactly what Christina would do, or would have to do for a living. That's why her heart broke when she awoke one morning to find her daughter's bed empty. Maria knew immediately where her daughter had gone. She also knew immediately what she must do to find her. She quickly threw some clothes in a bag, gathered up all her money, and ran out of the house.

On her way to the bus stop she entered a drugstore to get one last thing. Pictures. She sat in the photograph booth, closed the curtain, and spent all she could on pictures. With her purse full of small black and white photos, she boarded the next bus to Rio de Janeiro.

Maria knew that Christina had no way of earning money. She also knew that her daughter was too stubborn to give up. When pride meets hunger, a human will do things that were before unthinkable. Knowing this, Maria began her search. Bars, hotels, nightclubs, any place with the reputation for street walkers or prostitutes. She went to them all. And at each place she left her picture—taped to a bathroom mirror, tacked to a hotel bulletin board, fastened to a corner phone booth.

And on the back of each photo she wrote a note.

It wasn't too long before both the money and the pictures ran out, and Maria had to go home. The weary mother wept as the bus began its long journey back to her small village.

It was a few weeks later that young Christina descended the hotel stairs. Her young face was tired. Her brown eyes no longer danced with youth but spoke of pain and fear. Her laughter was broken. Her dream had become a nightmare. A thousand times over she had longed to trade these countless beds for her secure pallet. Yet the little village was, in too many ways, too far away.

As she reached the bottom of the stairs, her eyes noticed a familiar face. She looked again, and there on the lobby mirror was a small picture of her mother. Christina's eyes burned and her throat tightened as she walked across the room and removed the small photo. Written on the back was this compelling invitation: "Whatever you have done, whatever you have become, it doesn't matter. Please come home."

She did.

—*Max Lucado*
from No Wonder They
Call Him the Savior

Wealth

Measure wealth not by the things you have,
but by the things you have for which you
would not take money.

—Anonymous

My Two Sons

My two sons,
I always wanted you.
Even when I was a little girl
Playing with baby dolls.
I clothed them and fed them,
Rocked them and sang a lullaby.
Thinking that one day,
I would have babes of my own.

And God gave me you,
My two sons.
And I clothed you and fed you,
I rocked you to sleep
And sang you a lullaby.
And it was wonderful.
I wanted it to last
Forever.

But quickly you grew older,
With sturdy legs and grinning faces.
And we made a sandbox,
Played with Legos.
And read stories.
We learned to ride bikes,
And mended owies.
And you grew up.

Now you are young men.
Both over six feet tall,
with whiskers.
It feels like you don't need me—
very much.
And I have to let go.
And trust God to care for you,
But it's the hardest thing I've ever
done.

My two sons,
I always wanted you.
But now all I can do
Is watch and pray,
That you will let God
Clothe you, and feed you,
Rock you and sing you a lullaby.
And it will be wonderful.

—Melody Carlson
from *Stories for the*
Family's Heart

A Great Cup of Tea

I heard a story about a mother who was sick in bed with the flu. Her darling daughter wanted so much to be a good nurse. She fluffed the pillows and brought a magazine for her mother to read. And then she even showed up with a surprise cup of tea.

"Why, you're such a sweetheart," the mother said as she drank the tea. "I didn't know you even knew how to make tea."

"Oh, yes," the little girl replied. "I learned by watching you. I put the tea leaves in the pan and then I put in the water, and I boiled it, and then I strained it into a cup. But I couldn't find a strainer, so I used the flyswatter instead."

"You what?" the mother screamed.

And the little girl said, "Oh, don't worry, Mom, I didn't use the new flyswatter. I used the old one."

James Dobson
from Home with a Heart

Heirloom

It had belonged to Great-grandmother and he knew he must be very careful. The vase was one of mother's dearest treasures. She had told him so.

The vase, placed high on the mantel, was out of the reach of little hands, but somehow he managed. He just wanted to see if the tiny little rosebud border went all around the back. He didn't realize that a boy's five-year-old hands are sometimes clumsy and not meant to hold delicate porcelain treasures. It shattered when it hit the floor, and he began to cry. That cry soon became a sobbing wail, growing louder and louder. From the kitchen his mother heard her son crying and she came running. Her footsteps hurried down the hall and came around the corner. She stopped then, looked at him, and saw what he had done.

Between his sobs, he could hardly speak the words. "I broke...the vase."

And then his mother gave him a gift.

With a look of relief, his mother said, "Oh, thank heavens, I thought you were hurt!" And then she held him tenderly until his sobbing stopped.

She made it very clear—he was the treasure. Though now a grown man, it is a gift he still carries in his heart.

—*Ann Weems*
Retold by Alice Gray
from More Stories for the Heart

Tender Intuition

I hold you in my arms, young prince. You sleep in sweet, heavenly peace. Yet, I wonder if you'd be so calm if you knew the truth: I am your mother. And I don't have the slightest idea what I'm doing. You are my first baby ever. My only son. I was just getting used to being pregnant, and now here you are! And you are so very, very real.

I've been preparing for your arrival for months. I've read the books. Well, some of them. A few pages. I've listened to my friends who give me endless advice. They're all experienced, you know, because they have their own babies. But you're different. You're my baby. And they don't know a thing about you.

I do. I know all about the way you kick and wiggle. I've already memorized the way you smell, like a fresh-from-the-earth daffodil. I know about the way your lower lip quivers when you're about to cry. I know that your wispy hair is the most luxuriously soft thing that has ever touched my cheek.

Yet I admit, there's much I don't know. In the hospital I had to be instructed on how to nurse you. Yesterday my mother showed me how to bathe you in the sink. I don't have a clue how to clear up diaper rash. I get queasy at the sight of blood. I don't sew. I'm not good at salt dough maps. My math skills are atrocious. And you might as well know right up—that wiggly teeth give me the heebie-jeebies.

However, I am very good at baking cookies. I know how to make indoor tents on rainy days. And I have my father's wonderful sense of humor so I know how to laugh and how to make you laugh.

I'll sing you sweet songs in the night. I'll pray for you every day. I'll let you keep any animal you catch, as long as you can feed it. I'll call all your imaginary friends by their first names. I'll put love notes in your lunch box, and I'll swim in the ocean with you, even when I'm old....

Such secrets of motherhood can't be learned over coffee with friends. They can't be taught by a book, or even by trial and error. To me, these tender intuitions are what matter most. Eternal insights only a mother can know—when her baby is in her arms as you are now in mine. This is where the Lord will teach me how to mother you by heart.

— *Robin Jones Gunn*
from Mothering by Heart

Bus Stop

Jason, our youngest, has two goals in life. One is to have fun, and the other is to rest. He does both quite well. So I shouldn't have been surprised by what happened when I sent him to school one fall day.

As Jason headed off for the bus, I immediately busied myself, preparing for a full day. The knock on the door was a surprise and disruptive to my morning rhythm, which is not something I have a lot of. I flew to the door, jerked it open, only to find myself looking at Jason.

"What are you doing here?" I demanded.

"I've quit school," he boldly announced.

"Quit school?" I repeated in disbelief and at a decibel too high for human ears.

Swallowing once, I tried to remember some motherly psychology. But all that came to my mind was "A stitch in time saves nine" and "Starve a fever, feed a cold," or something like that. Somehow they didn't seem to apply to a six-year-old drop-out dilemma. So I questioned, "Why have you quit school?"

Without hesitation he proclaimed, "It's too long, it's too hard, and it's too boring!"

"Jason," I instantly retorted, "you have just described life. Get on the bus!"

—Patsy Clairmont
from God Uses Cracked Pots

Tenderness

Mother's arms are made for tenderness,
and sweet sleep blesses the child
who lies therein.

—Victor Hugo

Leaving Home

High school was over, and I'd been up almost all night, first saying good-bye to my few remaining high school friends and then packing for college myself. Now I sat at our old kitchen table with my mother, enjoying her famous pancakes one last time before climbing into my jam-packed car. As I sat at that table, a flood of emotions hit me.

My mother had purchased the table when I was five years old. It sat next to a large kitchen window, with a commanding view of the front yard. For more than a decade, it served as the unofficial meeting place of the Trent family. In grade school, I can remember sitting there at countless dinners. There would be us three boys laughing and chattering about our day, my mother and grandmother scurrying back and forth to keep bottomless plates filled, and my grandfather quietly presiding over the chaos.

In high school, that table became the place where I could sit with my mother, anytime, day or night. There she would patiently listen to whatever "crisis" or problem I was having in school or in dating. That old table proudly displayed birthday cards as we grew older and solemnly bore the flowers we brought home from the funeral home the day my grandfather was laid to rest.

Over the years, more chairs began to empty. My older brother, Joe, married and began a home of his own. My grandmother went to live with my aunt, and my twin brother, Jeff, left for a different college. Now it was down to just Mom and me, sitting at that table one last time.

I can remember how well I thought she was handling that morning. No tears. No dip in her always present smile. Just that nonstop encouragement that has calmed my fears since I was a child and always made me feel like I could accomplish anything I set my mind to. Things like driving a thousand miles by myself to a new college and making a new start without knowing a single person at an out-of-state school.

I finished breakfast, hugged the best mom in the world, and confidently strode to my '64 forest green Volkswagen. Every square inch was crammed with "important stuff" for college—everything from my legendary record collection to my new, seldom-used razor. I jumped inside the car, fired up the engine, and drove off with a wave and a smile. I was on my way! Nothing was going to stop me now! Nothing, that is, except driving into the rising sun that quickly made me realize I'd forgotten one thing—my sunglasses on the nightstand.

I turned the car around, drove back into the driveway, and walked in to find my mother still sitting at the kitchen table, crying. All morning she had kept a stiff upper lip, managing to hold her emotions in check at seeing her last son leave home. But when I walked back in the door unexpectedly, all that changed. There was an awkward silence, and then we both lost it. We sat at that table, crowded with memories, hugged each other, and cried and cried.

I can't explain exactly what happened that sun-splashed morning in the kitchen, but our relationship changed. There was no less love, no less caring, but somehow we both knew that this would be the last time I would sit down at that old kitchen table as a child.

—*John Trent*
from Love for All Seasons

First Words

"I shall miss Mother this Christmas," the clerk in the Asheville store told me. Her mother had died recently, and this would be the first Christmas without her.

"I used to go home in the evenings, and we'd have such good times together."

The day they put her in the hospital, the doctor told the children they would have to stay out of her room in order for her to rest and get adjusted.

"So I stayed out in the hall," she continued, "waiting...listening. Finally I could stand it no longer, and I went in.

" 'I thought you'd never come!' Mother said."

Blinking back the tears, the clerk added, with a smile, "You know, I'm thinking they'll be the first words she'll say to me when I get to Heaven!"

—*Ruth Bell Graham*
from Legacy of a Pack Rat

Just in Case

Living as we did in a congested and bustling city, my mother arranged with a teenage girl who lived next door to walk me home at the end of the day. For this arduous responsibility, the girl was paid five cents a day, or a grand total of a quarter a week. In second grade, I became irritated that our poor family was giving this neighbor girl so much money, and I offered a deal to my mom. "Look," I said, "I'll walk myself to school and, if you give me a nickel a week, I will be extra careful. You can keep the other twenty cents and we'll all be better off." I pleaded and begged, and eventually my mother gave in to my proposal. For the next two years I walked to and from school all by myself. It was an eight-block walk with many streets to cross, but I crossed them all with great care. I didn't talk to any strangers. I always kept on the appointed path. I always did as I promised and I did it alone—or at least I thought I did.

Years later when we were enjoying a family party, I bragged about my characteristic independence and, in a grandiose fashion, reminded my family of how I had been able to take care of myself even as a small boy. I recalled the arrangements for going to and from school that I had worked out with Mom. It was then that my mother laughed and told me the whole story. "Did you really think you were alone?" she asked. "Every morning when you left for school, I left with you. I walked behind you all the way. When you got out of school at 3:30 in the afternoon, I was there. I always kept myself hidden, but I was there and I followed you all the way home. I just wanted to be there for you in case you needed me."

Mom was always there for me....

—*Tony Campolo*
from What My Parents Did Right

Blessed

She is clothed with strength and dignity;
    she can laugh at the days to come.
She speaks with wisdom,
    and faithful instruction is on her tongue.
She watches over the affairs of her household
    and does not eat the bread of idleness.
Her children arise and call her blessed;
    her husband also, and he praises her:
"Many women do noble things,
    but you surpass them all."

Proverbs 31:25–29

Legacy of an Adopted Child

Once there were two women
who never knew each other.
One you do not remember,
the other you call Mother.
Two different lives shaped
to make your one.
One became your guiding star,
the other became your sun.

The first one gave you life,
and the second taught you to live it.
The first gave you a need for love,
the second was there to give it.
One gave you a nationality,
the other gave you a name.
One gave you a talent,
the other gave you an aim.

One gave you emotions,
the other calmed your fears.
One saw your first sweet smile,
the other dried your tears.
One sought for you a home
that she could not provide,
The other prayed for a child
and her hope was not denied.

And now you ask
through your tears—
The age-old question
through the years—
Heredity or environment,
which are you the product of—
Neither, my darling—neither...
Just two different kinds of love.

—Author unknown

Mother's Covers

When you were small
And just a touch away,
I covered you with blankets
Against the cool night air.

But now that you are tall
And out of reach,
I fold my hands
And cover you in prayer.

—Author unknown

A New Hat for Shane

The toddler cowboy boots were scuffed on both toes and creased at the heels. I vowed to bronze them someday as I packed them into the steamer trunk along with a well-worn Piglet and a handmade baby quilt. How I wished I had kept Shane's beige, felt cowboy hat that had slouched over his forehead. My mind flooded with memories as I leaned against the wall and remembered my son's growing-up years.

Shane's fondness for hats grew as he did. I recalled him as a toddler wearing a hat and reading upside-down Dr. Seuss books while sitting in his small-scale rocker. Shane alternated between a chocolate brown hobo hat, a red cowboy hat, and an oversized western hat that had long since lost its shape. Later, a multi-colored beanie was added to Shane's collection after he learned his Bible verses for the "Good News Club."

In elementary school, Shane created his own head covering for a Christmas performance. His shepherd headgear was fashioned by tying an arm cover from the plaid couch around his forehead with twine. In the years that followed, he sported softball helmets, tennis visors, ball caps, "I Love Fishing" hats, camouflage hunting caps and hard hats.

As Shane's taste in hats developed, so did his desire to make his own way. Once at a fifth-grade track meet, we watched the typical Oregon partly sunny sky succumb to rain. Determined not to let the inclement weather dampen my son's enthusiasm, I edged close to the track. When the gun sounded for Shane's heat, I shouted with gusto, "Go, Bobbalou!"

As he crossed the finish line, I whooped and hollered and patted him on the back. Although he had run well, Shane had a sullen look on his face. "Mom," he sternly admonished, "don't ever call me Bobbalou in public again."

Several months later, Shane called me into his room one night for a talk. As I sat down on his bed, he counseled me, "Mom, I don't want to hurt your feelings, but please don't sing 'All Aboard for Blanket Bay' to me at bedtime anymore. After all, I am in middle school now." Shane was growing up. I got that message loud and clear.

When the day arrived that I left him waving on the curb of a college 2,000 miles from home, I felt as if part of me had been amputated. I realized that my son would acquire strength only if I allowed him to exercise his power of choice. But knowing that did nothing to alleviate my fear that his decisions might cause him pain. The days of holding him on my lap and whispering words of comfort were gone. Instead, I had to release this one I loved so much to the One who loved him more.

Shane eventually chose a wife. She was from the mountains of Montana where real-life cowboys still make their living. It was no surprise to me that on his wedding day Shane wore a black tux with tails—and a new black Stetson. During the ceremony, Shane watched just inches from me as his bride approached on her father's arm. I wanted to reach out and squeeze his arm, but I resisted. I sensed this was a pivotal moment —a rite of passage for me as well as him.

As Shane confidently stepped forward and extended his arm to his bride, my heart constricted with emotions...pride and love for this precious son who was stepping into regions unknown with a new partner, and momentary sadness for our relationship which was from that moment altered forever.

As I watched Shane and his wife exchange their wedding vows, I consciously exchanged my role as his primary nurturer to that of their number one encourager. I sensed that only as I completely released my son to move forward with his life would I be freed to fully enter into the thrill of watching him grow into manhood. Shane indeed wore a new hat that day. And so, I realized, did I.

I sighed as I locked the trunk and returned it to storage. Someday I really will bronze those boots. And even though the old felt cowboy hat never found a place in the keepsake chest, it will always be a priceless symbol to me of a lifetime of growth—for my son and myself.

—Rhonda Wehler
from Stories for the Family's Heart

A Mother's Way

The young mother set her foot on the path of life. "Is the way long?"

"Yes," her Guide said, "and the way is hard. You will be old before you reach the end of it. But—" He stopped to smile warmly. "The end will be better than the beginning."

The young mother was so happy, though, that she could not believe anything could be better than these early years. She played with her children, and gathered flowers for them along the way, and bathed with them in the clear streams. The sun shone on them and life was good, and the young mother cried, "Nothing will ever be lovelier than this."

Then night came, and storm, and the path was dark. The children shook with fear and cold, and the mother drew them close, covering them with her mantle. Her children said, "Oh, Mother, we are not afraid when you are near." The mother said, "This is better than the brightness of day, for I have taught my children courage."

Then the morning came, and there was a hill ahead. The children climbed and grew weary. The mother was weary, too, but she kept encouraging her children, "A little patience and we are there." So the children continued to climb. When they reached the top, they said, "We could not have done it without you, Mother." And the mother, when she lay down that night, looked past the stars and said, "This is a better day than the last. My children have learned fortitude in the face of difficulty. Yesterday I taught them courage, today I have taught them strength."

With the next day came strange clouds that darkened the earth—clouds of war and hate and evil. The children groped and stumbled. The mother said, "Look up. Lift your eyes past the blackness to the Light." The children looked up and saw an Everlasting Glory above the strange clouds. It guided them and brought them through the darkness and evil. That night the mother said, "This is the best day of all, for I have helped my children learn to see God."

The days went on, and the weeks and the months and the years. The mother grew old, until she was very little and bent. But her children were tall and strong, and they walked with courage. When the way was hard, they helped their mother; when the way was rough, they lifted her, for she was as light as a feather. At last they came to a hill, and beyond the hill they could see a shining road and golden gate flung wide.

The mother said, "I have reached the end of my journey. Now I know that the end really is better than the beginning, for my children can walk alone, and they will teach their children after them."

The children said, "You will always walk with us, Mother, even when you have gone through the gates."

They stood and watched her as she went on alone, and the gates closed after her. They said, "We can't see her, but she is with us still. A mother like ours is more than a memory."

—*Temple Bailey*

OTHER BOOKS COMPILED BY ALICE GRAY

Stories for the Heart
More Stories for the Heart
Christmas Stories for the Heart
Stories for the Family's Heart
Keepsakes for the Heart – Friendship

KEEPSAKES FOR THE HEART—MOTHER
published by Multnomah Publishers, Inc.

© 1998 by Multnomah Publishers, Inc.
International Standard Book Number: 1-57673-384-X

All photographs © by David Bailey, except page 24 © by Claudia Kunin.
Book Design by Kevin Keller and Holly Davison
Printed in China

Unless otherwise indicated, Scripture quotations are from the
New International Version © 1973, 1984 by International Bible Society
used by permission of Zondervan Publishing House

Multnomah is a trademark of Multnomah Publishers, Inc., and is registered
in the U.S. Patent and Trademark Office.

Every effort has been made to provide proper and accurate source attribution
for selections in this volume. Should any attribution be found to be incorrect,
the publisher welcomes written documentation supporting correction for
subsequent printings. For material not in the public domain, selections
were made according to generally accepted fair-use standards and
practices. The publisher gratefully acknowledges the cooperation of
publishers and individuals granting permission for use of longer selections;
please see the acknowledgments for full attribution of these sources.

   For information:
MULTNOMAH PUBLISHERS, INC.
POST OFFICE BOX 1720
SISTERS, OREGON 97759

98 99 00 01 02 03—7 6 5 4 3 2 1

ACKNOWLEDGMENTS

Grateful acknowledgment is given to all who have contributed to this book. Any inadvertent omissions of credit will be gladly corrected in future editions.

"When You Thought I Wasn't Looking" by Mary Rita Schilke Korzan, Granger, Ind., © 1980. This poem is now matted and available for distribution by the author. It was inspired by Mary's mother, Blanche Schilke. Used by permission.

"Mother Earned Her Wrinkles" by Erma Bombeck from *Forever Erma* ©1996 by the estate of Erma Bombeck, Universal Press Syndicate. Used by permission. All rights reserved.

"Act of Love" by Alice Gray from *Stories for the Heart* (Sisters, Ore.: Multnomah Publishers, Inc., 1996). Used by permission.

"The Nest" by Evelyn Petty ©1997. Used by permission.

"Come Home" by Max Lucado from *No Wonder They Call Him the Savior* (Sisters, Ore.: Multnomah Publishers, Inc., 1986). Used by permission.

"My Two Sons" by Melody Carlson © 1997. Used by permission.

"A Great Cup of Tea" by James Dobson from *Home with a Heart* (Wheaton, Ill.: Tyndale House Publishers, Inc., 1996). All rights reserved.

"Heirloom" by Ann Weems, retold by Alice Gray from *More Stories for the Heart* (Sisters, Ore.: Multnomah Publishers, Inc., 1997). Used by permission.

"Tender Intuition" by Robin Jones Gunn from *Mothering by Heart* (Sisters, Ore.: Multnomah Publishers, Inc., 1996). Used by permission.

"Bus Stop" by Patsy Clairmont from *God Uses Cracked Pots* (Colorado Springs, Colo.: Focus on the Family, 1991). Used by permission. All rights reserved. International copyright secured.

"Leaving Home" by John Trent from *Love for All Seasons* (Chicago, Ill.: Moody Press, 1996). Used by permission.

"First Words" by Ruth Bell Graham from *Legacy of a Pack Rat* (Nashville, Tenn.: Thomas Nelson, 1989). Used by permission.

"Just in Case" by Tony Campolo from *What My Parents Did Right* (Wheaton, Ill.: Tyndale House Publishers, Inc., 1994). Used by permission.

"A New Hat for Shane" by Rhonda Wehler ©1996. Used by permission. Also published in *Single Parent Family*, 1996.

"A Mother's Way" by Temple Bailey. Original source unknown.